INDONESIA ENERGY SECTOR ASSESSMENT, STRATEGY, AND ROAD MAP

UPDATE

DECEMBER 2020

ASIAN DEVELOPMENT BANK

ADB

Note:
In this publication, "$" refers to United States dollars.

Cover design by Cleone Baradas.

Contents

Tables and Figure   iv

Acknowledgments   v

Abbreviations   vi

Weights and Measures   vi

Currency Equivalents   vi

Sector Assessment: Context and Strategic Issues   1
    Introduction   1
    Overall Sector Context   1
    Energy in Focus   2
    Institutional Context   6
    Core Sector Issues   8

Sector Strategy   22
    Government Strategy, Policy, and Plans   22
    ADB Sector Support Program and Experience   23
    Other Development Partner Support   24
    ADB Sector Forward Strategy   26

Energy Sector Road Map and Results Framework   28

Appendix: Problem Tree for the Energy Sector   29

Tables and Figure

Tables

1   Network Development Planning   12
2   ADB Major Public Sector Projects in Indonesia Since 2016   23
3   ADB Major Private Sector Projects in Indonesia Since 2016   23
4   Major Development Partners and Programs 2016–2019   24

Figure

1   Primary Energy Supply, 2019   4

Acknowledgments

The report was written by Florian Kitt (energy specialist, Energy Division, Southeast Asia Department) and Kelsey Yates (consultant, ADB). Additional guidance and support were provided by Toru Kubo (director, Energy Division, Southeast Asia Department). Additional support was provided by Divya Nawale (consultant, ADB). The team wishes to thank Yongping Zhai (chief, Energy Sector Group, Sustainable Development and Climate Change Department) as the report's peer reviewer.

The team wishes to thank the Ministry of Energy and Mineral Resources, BAPPENAS, PT PLN, and development partners for data and inputs during the preparation of the report. The team also thanks colleagues from the Indonesia Resident Mission and the Department of Communications for their support.

Director	Toru Kubo, Energy Division, Southeast Asia Department (SERD)
Team leader	Florian Kitt, energy specialist, SERD
Team member	Jeffrey Almera, senior operations assistant, SERD
Peer reviewer	Yongping Zhai, chief, Energy Sector Group, Sustainable Development and Climate Change Department

Abbreviations

ADB	Asian Development Bank
ASR	assessment, strategy, and road map
BAPPENAS	Badan Perencanaan Pembangunan Nasional (Ministry of National Development Planning)
CO2	carbon dioxide
COVID-19	coronavirus disease
CPS	country partnership strategy
ESCO	energy service company
GDP	gross domestic product
IPP	independent power producer
KEN	Kebijakan Energi Nasional (National Energy Policy)
LED	light-emitting diode
LNG	liquefied natural gas
LPG	liquefied petroleum gas
MEMR	Kementerian Energi dan Sumber Daya Mineral (Ministry of Energy and Mineral Resources)
MOF	Ministry of Finance
PPA	power purchase agreement
PPP	public-private partnership
PLN	Perusahaan Listrik Negara (State Electricity Corporation)
RPJMN	Nasional Rencana Pembangunan Jangka Menengah (National Medium-Term Development Plan)
RUEN	National Energy Plan
RUKN	Rencana Umum Keternagalistrikan Nasional (National General Plan for Electricity)
RUPTL	Rencana Usaha Penyediaan Tenaga Listrik (Electricity Power Supply Business Plan)
SOE	state-owned enterprise

Weights and Measures

GW	gigawatt
MVA	megavolt-ampere
MW	megawatt
TWh	terawatt-hour

Currency Equivalents

(as of 24 November 2020)

Currency unit	–	rupiah (Rp)
Rp1.00	=	$0.000071
$1.00	=	Rp14.149

Sector Assessment: Context and Strategic Issues

Introduction

This energy sector assessment, strategy, and road map (ASR) updates the state of the energy sector in the Republic of Indonesia since the 2016 publication of Indonesia Energy Sector Assessment, Strategy and Review by the Asian Development Bank (ADB). This ASR aims to provide background information and an overview of past and ongoing successes and constraints in ADB development areas in order to support investment and technical assistance operations in Indonesia's energy sector. This will assist in following ADB's country partnership strategy (CPS) for Indonesia.

The CPS sets out the principles for the assistance and partnership between ADB and the Government of Indonesia. The CPS is aligned with the government's policies and priorities in its National Medium-Term Development Plan (RPJMN), 2020–2024. It focuses on three strategic pathways: (i) improving well-being; (ii) accelerating economic recovery; and (iii) strengthening resilience. Indonesia has identified knowledge needs in these areas, including transformative strategies for recovery from the adverse impact of the coronavirus disease (COVID-19) pandemic and building resilience to exogenous shocks. Furthermore, the ASR draws upon ADB's Strategy 2030, which outlines a framework for ADB's overall operations.[1]

Overall Sector Context

Indonesia is a large archipelago comprising more than 17,000 islands, which stretch 5,000 kilometers across Southeast Asia and Oceania. Indonesia shares land borders with Papua New Guinea, Timor-Leste, and Malaysia, and maritime borders with Singapore, the Philippines, and Australia. With an estimated population of 269 million, Indonesia is the fourth most populous country in the world.[2] More than half the population lives on the island of Java, where economic activity is concentrated, while the rest is spread across Sumatra, Bali, Sulawesi, Kalimantan, Nusa Tenggara, Maluku, Papua, and about 6,000 smaller inhabited islands. Indonesia has successfully reduced the extreme poverty level from 11.5% in 2015 to 9.4% in 2019, but the country's island geography makes sustainable economic and infrastructure development challenging in outlying provinces, resulting in persistent regional inequalities.[3]

---

[1] ADB. 2018. *Strategy 2030: Achieving a Prosperous, Inclusive, Resilient, and Sustainable Asia and the Pacific.* Manila.
[2] Statistics Indonesia. 2020. *Total Population Projection Result by Province and Gender (Thousand People), 2018–2020.* Jakarta.
[3] ADB. 2020. *Poverty Data: Indonesia.* Manila.

Indonesia is the largest economy in Southeast Asia and the seventh largest global economy in terms of purchasing power. Indonesia's gross domestic product (GDP) has increased steadily at approximately 5% per year from Rp861.9 billion in 2015 to more than Rp1 trillion in 2019.[4] Commodity and agriculture production has traditionally driven economic growth. Combined with government initiatives to invest in domestic infrastructure, the country's young, working-age population has enjoyed an increasingly higher standard of living in recent history. In 2019, manufacturing contributed 19.7% to GDP while services contributed 44.2%.[5] Progress was reflected in Indonesia's ease of doing business ranking rising from 120 in 2014 to 73 in 2019, while the index's subcomponent on electricity access improved from 122 to 33.[6]

Indonesia has made remarkable strides in political and economic development in the 21st century. It is now an upper-middle-income country aiming to achieve high-income country status by 2045. Despite substantial progress, however, the COVID-19 pandemic has had a severe human and economic impact, with 2020 growth forecast to contract for the first time since the Asian financial crisis in 1997. Since the onset of the pandemic, close to 10 million people have been placed at risk of falling below the national poverty line. Poverty incidence is expected to increase to between 11.9% and 12.8% in 2020.[7] The deterioration of the labor market will be felt disproportionately by the most vulnerable, including informal sector workers, who account for 57% of the labor force, adding to increased income inequality, which has been rising since 2009.[8] Economic growth is forecast to pick up in 2021, thanks to more robust household discretionary spending, an improved investment climate, and a recovery in the global economy. The risk of multiple COVID-19 waves and the speed at which the global economy and external demand recover however is difficult to predict.[9]

Energy in Focus

Energy is crucial to Indonesia's economy, and sustainable and equitable development of the sector is key to growth of the country. Indonesia is rich in commodity resources, particularly coal, natural gas, metals, and other mining and agricultural products. In 2019, the country produced 616 million tons of coal, 2.8 million standard cubic feet of natural gas and 272 million barrels of oil.[10] Indonesia is a net energy exporter, and the energy sector and overall economy has been built on natural resource extraction, with coal being Indonesia's principal export (11.2% of total energy export value) and palm oil second (8.76%).[11]

Energy is critical to economic development yet unreliable data, conflicting national policies, and prevailing organizational structures result in sector constraints. While national electrification rates have successfully increased, infrastructure may not be able to keep up with future regional demand. Necessary national generation capacity additions until 2025 are estimated to cost $154 billion, but securing financing poses a challenge following the impact of COVID-19 on public sector revenues. The first administration of President Joko Widodo, elected in 2014, began electricity tariff subsidy reform and eased access to capital for the private sector by establishing

---

4   ADB. 2020. *Basic Statistics, Asia and the Pacific*. Manila.
5   World Bank Data. 2020.
6   World Bank Group. 2015. *Doing Business 2014. Economy Profile Indonesia*. Washington DC; and World Bank Group. 2020. *Doing Business 2019. Economy Profile Indonesia*. Washington, DC.
7   ADB. 2020. *COVID-19 Active Response and Expenditure Support Program: Poverty Impact Assessment*. Jakarta.
8   Statistics Indonesia. 2020. *Labor Force Situation in Indonesia: February 2020*. Jakarta.
9   ADB. 2020. *Asian Development Outlook 2020 Supplement: Lockdown, Loosening, and Asia's Growth Prospects*. Manila.
10 Government of Indonesia, MEMR. 2020. *Handbook of Energy & Economic Statistics of Indonesia 2019*. Jakarta.
11 Statistics Indonesia. 2020. *Indonesia Foreign Trade Statistics Exports 2019*. Jakarta.

a legal basis for open access to transmission lines and a credit guarantee program to mitigate risks for electricity projects. More however needs to be done. A forthcoming presidential regulation is expected to introduce supportive frameworks to address key issues in the energy sector to ensure a green recovery from COVID-19.[12]

The COVID-19 pandemic presents a major shock to the energy sector. The State Electricity Corporation (PLN) faces a 15% decrease in electricity demand in 2020, while a depreciation of the Indonesian rupiah has increased the cost of US dollar-linked electricity generation, and made its foreign currency-denominated debt (68% of total) more costly. In addition, the government expanded electricity subsidies to protect the poorest 31 million households. Combined, this led to a 2020 first quarter loss of $2.8 billion for PLN, which decreased its investment planning by 50%. The energy outlook for 2021 is expected to improve as Indonesia returns to pre-COVID-19 economic growth levels. The energy sector facilitated Indonesia's COVID-19 response and will be key in its economic recovery. Uninterrupted energy supply enabled hospitals to provide care, food to be delivered, and people to work from home. Without the provision of reliable and affordable electricity to its population, the COVID-19 lockdowns would have resulted in far greater economic damage.[13] In addition to achieving carbon dioxide (CO_2) emission reductions, future clean energy infrastructure investment offers high returns by driving down costs and can deliver high multipliers for the recovery due to its labor intensity.[14]

Energy Resources

As of 2019, nonrenewable energy resources are coal at 149 billion tons proven with 37.6 billon tons of potential reserves; oil at 2.48 billion barrels proven, within an additional 1.29 billion barrels potential; and natural gas at 49.74 billion barrels proven and 27.55 billion barrels potential (footnote 10). The government estimates that the country has the largest global potential for geothermal energy at 23.9 gigawatts (GW) and potential for hydropower of more than 94 GW (footnote 10). The country also has a biomass potential of more than 32.6 GW and a biogas potential of 200,000 barrels per day.[15] Projections for renewable energies are estimated at 60.6 GW for wind energy, 208 GW for solar energy, and 17.9 GW for ocean and tidal energy.[16] With rapidly advancing renewable energy technology, the potential could be substantially larger.

Energy Balance

The government's overall strategy for its energy sector emphasizes diversification, environmental sustainability, and maximum use of domestic energy resources. The National Energy Policy (KEN) 2014 targets a primary energy mix of 23% new and renewable energy, 22% gas, 55% coal, and 0.4% oil by 2025. The National Electricity Plan (RUKN) aims at a long-term goal of 28% new and renewable energy, 25% gas, 47% coal, and 0.1% oil for electricity usage. Additionally, energy efficiency measures target the reduction of energy consumption by 1% per year.

As depicted in Figure 1, Indonesia's primary energy supply mix in 2019 consisted of oil 35%, coal 37.3%, gas 18.5%, hydropower 2.5%, geothermal 1.7%, biofuel 3%, and biogas, solar, wind, and other renewables at nearly 2%. Final energy consumption by sector is split into 44% transportation, 37% industry, 14% households, 4.5% commercial, and the rest to other (footnote 10).

---

12 Institute for Energy Economics and Financial Analysis. 2020. *Indonesian Government Pushing Ahead with Reforms to Jump-Start Renewable Energy Transition*. Jakarta.
13 International Energy Agency (IEA). 2020. *Sustainable Recovery*. Paris.
14 Smith School of Enterprise and the Environment. 2020. *Will COVID-19 Fiscal Recovery Packages Accelerate or Retard Progress on Climate Change?* Oxford.
15 BP. 2019. *BP Statistical Review of World Energy, 68th edition*. London.
16 Government of Indonesia, MEMR. 2019. *Indonesia Energy Outlook 2019*. Jakarta.

Figure 1: Primary Energy Supply, 2019

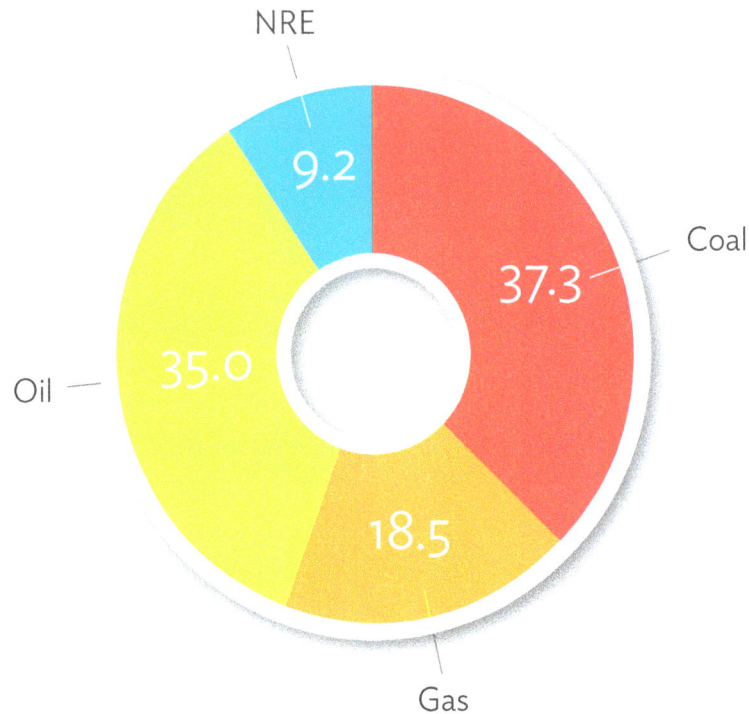

NRE = new and renewable energy (includes hydropower, geothermal, biofuel, biogas, solar, wind, and other renewables).
Source: Government of Indonesia, Ministry of Energy and Mineral Resources. 2020. Handbook of Energy & Economic Statistics of Indonesia 2019. Jakarta.

Energy Demand

Primary energy demand has increased by 3% per year since 2010, predominantly due to growth in the transport sector resulting in higher consumption of oil products including gasoline, diesel, and jet fuel.[17] Indonesia's energy consumption rose from 2.85 barrels of oil equivalent (BOE) per capita in 2016 to 3.53 BOE per capita in 2019 (footnote 10). Primary energy supply is projected to be 314 million tons of oil equivalent in 2025 and 943 million tons of oil equivalent in 2050 under a business-as-usual scenario (footnote 15).

In terms of electricity, the islands of Bali, Java, and Madura together had an estimated demand for 181 terawatt-hours (TWh) in 2019, followed by Sumatra, which forecast 38 TWh of electricity demand for 2019 (footnote 17). The 2019 estimated demand for Kalimantan, Sulawesi, Maluku, and Papua was 24 TWh (footnote 17). Electricity demand is expected to increase particularly from the industrial and household sectors. Indonesia's Electricity Power Supply Business Plan (RUPTL) 2019–2028 estimated annual electricity demand to increase by 6.4% through 2019–2028. Actual demand growth however was 4.5% in 2019 and 2.8% in January 2020. Furthermore, PLN has reduced its 2020 revenue target by 14.6%, due to decrease in demand caused by the COVID-19 pandemic.[18]

---

17   Enerdata. 2020. *Indonesia Energy Information*. Grenoble.
18   Powerline. 2020. *Indonesian Utility PLN Reduces its 2020 Revenue-Target Due to COVID-19 Impact*. New Delhi.

Over the past 5 years, optimistic government plans and corresponding electricity demand forecasts have not aligned with actual economic growth, resulting in over-investment in PLN capacity. The RUPTL 2019–2028 indicates that overcapacity in the Java-Bali system will last at least until 2026, and now probably much longer given the acute impact of COVID-19.

Climate Change

Indonesia is one of the most natural disaster-prone countries in the world, making the nation particularly vulnerable to climate change.[19] Indonesia is especially exposed to sea-level rise, with the country ranked the fifth highest in terms of population inhabiting the lower elevation coastal zone.[20] Currently, Indonesia is the 10th largest greenhouse gas emitting country and 19th highest country in terms of CO_2 emissions per capita.[21] Deforestation contributes significantly to greenhouse gas emissions, but emissions from energy use and agriculture are increasing. In 2017, 38.3% of greenhouse gas emissions came from energy systems.[22] While climate change will impact infrastructure across sectors, energy systems are particularly vulnerable.

Under the United Nations Framework Convention on Climate Change (UNFCCC) Paris Climate Agreement, the government has committed to reducing greenhouse gas emissions unconditionally by 29% against a business-as-usual scenario, and, with international assistance, by up to 41% against the 2030 business-as-usual scenario.[23] Recognizing that its economic growth goals will depend on its ability to harness sufficient sustainable and reliable energy sources and reduce emissions, the government has launched various plans since 2014. In 2017, the Ministry of National Development Planning (BAPPENAS) integrated climate action into the country's development agenda by launching a low-carbon initiative with an outline plan including three emission pathways through to 2045 (footnote 22).

The extraction of fossil fuels and natural resources is essential to providing Indonesia's primary energy supply, which increases the vulnerability of the sector as well as the economy. Since Indonesia's energy mix is highly dependent on fossil fuels and polluting, it both directly contributes to and is threatened by climate change. Extraction of fossil fuels and water for steam production in coal and gas power plants and for cooling degrades land and threatens water supplies already vulnerable to weather patterns changing due to global warming. Although new targets aim to diversify the energy resource mix to include less natural resource-dependent sources, shifting to new and renewable energy has been slow and is also at risk due to climate change itself. Shifts in rainfall and river discharge patterns will impact hydroelectric power production, the largest renewable electricity source in Indonesia. Biomass feedstock cultivation is vulnerable too, due to rising temperatures and land degradation.

In 2019, the government made significant progress in outlining the implementation of projects to address climate change and transform the energy sector. Aspirational plans for more than 17 GW of renewable energy additions over the next 10 years and the mandate of 20% biofuel blend are outlined in PLN's RUPTL 2019–2028. The country has adopted a Geothermal Resource Risk Mitigation program,[24] and introduced two regulations to ease the development of rooftop,[25] and floating solar projects.[26] The first utility-scale wind and solar power plants have also

[19] Global Facility for Disaster Reduction and Recovery. 2020. *Country Profile Indonesia*. Washington, DC.
[20] Neumann, B., Vafeidis, A. T., Zimmermann, J., & Nicholls, R. J. 2015. Future Coastal Population Growth and Exposure to Sea-Level Rise and Coastal Flooding: A Global Assessment. PLOS ONE. 10 (3).
[21] IEA. 2020. *Emissions from Fuel Combustion 2019 Highlights*. Paris.
[22] Government of Indonesia, BAPPENAS. 2020. *Indonesia Low Carbon Development Plan*. Jakarta.
[23] Government of Indonesia. 2016. *First Nationally Determined Contribution, Republic of Indonesia*. Jakarta.
[24] World Bank Group. 2019. *Indonesia: Scaling Up Geothermal Energy by Reducing Exploration Risks*. Washington, DC.
[25] Government of Indonesia, MEMR. 2019. *Ministerial Regulation No. 16/2019*. Jakarta.
[26] Government of Indonesia, Ministry of Public Works and Housing. 2020. *Ministerial Regulation No. 6/2020*. Jakarta.

been constructed.[27] To support the development of sustainable transport, the first mass rapid transit system opened in Jakarta in 2019, and the government mandated the development and production of domestic electric vehicle infrastructure.[28]

Institutional Context

Government Institutions

The agency principally responsible for governing the Indonesian energy sector is the Ministry of Energy and Mineral Resources (MEMR). MEMR comprises directorate generals focusing on oil and gas, minerals and coal, electricity, and new and renewable energies and energy conservation. The MEMR is the primary government institution in charge of policy and decision-making concerning Indonesia's energy and mining assets, including implementation of technical programs and projects. MEMR is responsible for preparing the National Energy Plan (RUEN) and the RUKN.

The MEMR and its Directorate General of Electricity and the Directorate General of New and Renewable Energy and Energy Conservation regulate the power sector. The MEMR is also primarily responsible for collecting and publishing national energy data.

The Directorate General of Oil and Gas is the regulator charged with governance of the oil and gas market in Indonesia, including policy and regulation setting. The subsector is split into upstream and mid- and downstream activities. The Special Task Force for Upstream Oil and Natural Gas Business Activities manages exploration and production contracts, while the Regulatory Body for Downstream Oil and Natural Gas Business Activities regulates mid- and downstream activities.

The National Energy Council brings together seven ministries and energy sector stakeholders to produce the KEN, approve the RUEN, and establish the framework to deal with crisis conditions and energy emergencies.[29] The Coordinating Ministry for Maritime and Investment Affairs is the coordination body for energy across ministries.

Other relevant ministries include BAPPENAS, which prepares Indonesia's RPJMN. This plan guides government programs and budgeting in general, and provides for national development activities relating to energy supply and demand. The Ministry of Finance (MOF) determines and administers the budget allocation, approved by the People's Representative Council, for state expenditures for MEMR including allocating energy subsidies, government guarantees, and tax regimes for energy products, infrastructure, and operations.

Several other government agencies and ministries regulate compliance with energy sector laws and policies. The Ministry of Public Works and Public Housing regulates water use rights, including water use taxes that are part of the operating costs absorbed by hydropower plants. The Ministry of Environment and Forestry approves access

---

27 ADB. 2018. *ADB Finances First Ever Utility-Scale Solar PV Plants in Indonesia in $160 Million Renewables Deal*. Manila.
28 Government of Indonesia. 2019. *Presidential Decree No 55/2019*. Jakarta.
29 These are the Ministry of Finance, BAPPENAS, Ministry of Transportation, Ministry of Industry, Ministry of Agriculture, Ministry of Technology Research and Higher Education, Ministry of Environment and Forestry; Ministry of Energy and Mineral Resources, and Directorate General of Electricity.

to forest land for geothermal projects, hydropower projects, and transmission and distribution lines. Additionally, this ministry establishes and enforces environmental standards and regulations for resource extraction and energy production. The Ministry of State-Owned Enterprises is responsible for the corporate governance of state-owned enterprises (SOEs), including those associated with energy. The ministry functions as the government's shareholder representative for national SOEs.

State-Owned Enterprises

SOEs are at least 51% government-owned corporations. They play a primary role throughout the entire energy value chain in Indonesia. They are established to either make a profit or to serve social functions. The government may also assign profit-seeking SOEs mandates to work toward the goals and needs of the state; where such mandates are not commercially feasible, such as selling electricity below the cost of the supply, the government is legally obliged to compensate the SOE for conducting that function.

Although private firms participate in both upstream exploration and production as well as downstream product retailing, PT Pertamina functions as the holding company for all oil and gas SOEs and dominates both the upstream and downstream segments. For electricity, PLN acts as a single buyer and owns more than two-thirds of generation and virtually all network infrastructure. As of 2016, the government can extend sovereign guarantees as required by most international development finance institutions to facilitate direct lending to infrastructure SOEs.[30]

The government approved the merger of PT Perusahaan Gas Negara and Pertamina in 2018, appointing Pertamina as the majority shareholder and further extending its dominance in the oil and gas midstream sector.[31] Through its subsidiaries, Pertamina is the largest single gas producer and is expected to soon become the largest oil producer. In particular, this merger was intended to streamline and accelerate the planning and construction of gas pipelines throughout the country. Pertamina also operates seven out of nine refineries in the country. Its business operations encompass oil and gas exploration and production, liquefied natural gas (LNG) development and marketing, geothermal, compressed natural gas, and coalbed methane. Pertamina has operations in more than 12 countries.

PLN functions as a single buyer. Its 2019 revenues, including subsidies and other government compensation, was Rp277 trillion, and it had total fixed assets of over Rp1.2 quadrillion.[32] With more than 75 million customers, it is one of the largest electric utilities in the world (footnote 32). PLN owns and operates all transmission, distribution, and retail sales throughout the country except where the government has specifically permitted other companies to provide these functions, such as a few dozen industrial estates. PLN has approximately 67 subsidiaries and joint venture companies, including generation subsidiaries. PLN prepares the RUPTL annually for approval by MEMR. The RUPTL presents a demand forecast and a transmission and generation expansion plan to meet this future demand, but these capacity additions are often not implemented as planned.

Private Sector

Private sector participation is crucial to Indonesia's energy sector growth, especially since many of the SOEs are experiencing financial constraints. Private companies accounted for 30% of funding for Indonesia's power sector

---

30 Government of Indonesia. 2016. *Presidential Regulation 44/2016*. Jakarta.
31 Government of Indonesia, Indonesia Investment Coordinating Board. *Regulation 6/2018*. Jakarta.
32 PLN. 2020. *PLN Statistics 2019*. Jakarta.

from 2016 till 2019; with export credit agencies and development financial institutions accounting for 40%.[33] The private sector is involved in nearly every segment of the power generation value chain and is responsible for the majority of both oil and gas production. In terms of electricity, 27% of all electricity was generated by independent power producers (IPPs) and private power utilities in 2019, increasing from 25% in 2014 (footnote 32). The government has a particular interest in private sector involvement in order to achieve the economies of scale required to reduce the cost of renewable and sustainable sources of energy.

Indonesia recognizes the importance of private companies in the energy sector. However, frequent changes in policy result in a lack of regulatory certainty, which impedes domestic and foreign IPPs and other participants from entering the Indonesian energy market.[34] Public finance was expected to provide 51% of the funding needed for the $154 billion of investment required for energy infrastructure through 2025. For 2020, the government had budgeted only one-fifth of the $803 million needed before the pandemic began, and has reduced state investments by half since (footnote 34). The private sector will therefore be needed to meet financing goals. Key issues such as uncertainties in licensing, land procurement, electricity grid access, data and projections, tariff pricing, contract clauses, and diverging central and regional licensing processes have reinforced the lack of private sector investment and future commitments for sustainable energy projects.

Efforts are underway to promote private sector participation in the energy sector through private-public partnership (PPP) mechanisms. The 2GW Batang Central Java Coal Power Plant, which was identified as a PPP project in 2005 and is expected to operate this year, is the first PPP project in Indonesia's energy sector. A 12-city Waste to Energy Development Plan and a Gas Distribution Network Development Plan are also expected to use PPP mechanisms.[35] The MOF intends to provide subsidies and extend a project development facility to realize these plans. Furthermore, as a PPP promotion activity, MOF plans to budget Rp5.9 trillion for project development facility activity and Rp64.4 trillion in a viability gap funding subsidy for 2020–2024.[36] The MOF is working with international institutions, including ADB, to ensure support to government contracting agencies in preparing PPP projects, which should enhance the agencies' capabilities in attracting private sector involvement in PPPs.

Core Sector Issues

Many electricity sector policies awaiting implementing rules and regulations are not aligned with each other, or contradict related non-energy regulations. Several official plans, including RUEN, RUPTL, and RUKN, rely on unrealistic data input assumptions, and provide conflicting and unachievable targets. Due to incorrect baseline emissions figures and overly optimistic economic growth assumptions, Indonesia's nationally determined contributions under the Paris agreement imply that Indonesia could actually increase its rate of growth in carbon intensity and emissions significantly and still achieve its absolute required reductions. Indonesia has been working to improve the reliability of MEMR's energy data and strengthened its regulatory review process to ensure consistency between regulations.

Fossil fuel dominates primary energy, despite a declaration in the 2014 RUEN that Indonesia would work to maximize the share of renewable energy while optimizing gas and minimizing oil and coal as the baseload to

---

[33] IEA. 2020. *Attracting Private Investment to Fund Sustainable Recoveries: The Case of Indonesia's Power Sector*. Paris.

[34] ADB. 2020. *Independent Assessment of Indonesia's Energy Infrastructure Sector*. Manila.

[35] Government of Indonesia. 2018. *Presidential Regulation No. 35/2018*. Jakarta.

[36] Komite Percepatan Penyediaan Infrastruktur Prioritas. 2020. Batang Power Plant. Jakarta.

fulfill the remaining energy needs. According to projections, the use of fossil fuels will rise steadily through 2045. Extractive fuels are threatening not only human health and biodiversity but also growing economic sectors such as tourism.[37] Current policies such as price caps on coal, growth key performance indicators, unrealistic reserve margins, and other domestic obligations have resulted in fossil fuels such as coal and natural gas to be artificially more financially attractive than lower-emission options, resulting in PLN entering into fixed long-term contracts with these sources. The growing share of coal in the primary energy supply is not only contributing to environmental degradation, but there is no mechanism to ensure that Natural Resource Profit Sharing Funds are provided to provincial regencies to directly benefit the local communities where the resource is extracted.

Rapid urbanization in regions with inefficient public transport has increased reliance on petrol for personal cars and motorbikes. Poorly targeted fuel subsidies remain for highly polluting options such as subgrade fuels, sustaining reliance on these highly polluting options. In metropolitan regions, the increased use of these fuels, combined with proximity to coal-fired generation, has resulted in worsening air quality that threatens health and the environment.

Indonesia has an abundance of renewable energy resources, but impediments inhibit greater uptake of these resources. Roadblocks in the prevailing institutional frameworks, particularly around restrictive rules regarding procurement and implementation, prevent Indonesia from developing a low-cost renewable energy market at any scale. Indonesia has the highest financing costs of renewable energy projects in the region due to uncertain and unbalanced contract risk allocation, including the practice of renegotiating contracts and power purchase agreements (PPA), design, stringent local content requirements, and risks from inexperienced renewable energy developers. Private and foreign companies and capital would help bridge the gap, yet they are dissuaded from entering due to the unstable policy and regulatory environment. For example, eight different geothermal pricing regulations have been issued over the past 11 years. In 2017, MEMR reversed years of prorenewable energy policies through a series of regulations that introduced policies such as tariff setting based on the average cost of electricity supply, take-and-pay contracts, and a requirement to build-own-operate-transfer, which adversely affected the bankability of PPAs (footnote 34).[38] Furthermore, nonstringent emission standards for fossil fuel power plants and an abundance of low-cost coal resulted in an expansion of coal-fired generation by 5 GW between 2015 and 2018. This displaced cleaner least cost alternatives, as PLN cancelled the majority of the 70 renewable energy PPAs signed in 2017. Without significant progress in capacity additions, Indonesia is at risk of failing to meet its renewable energy target of 23% of primary energy agreed upon in the 2014 RUEN.

Energy efficiency and renewable energy go hand in hand in reducing CO_2 emissions and planning for energy development, yet they are vastly underused in Indonesia. Energy efficiency would reduce energy generation emissions and required generation capacity, but existing regulations are ineffective or non-existent for this market. Energy efficient measures have not taken off due to low energy pricing, poor enforcement of existing regulations, lack of financing and insufficient energy conservation guidelines, which has hindered the development of an energy auditing and energy service company industry.

Many SOEs are financially strained. Tariffs do not reflect true energy prices, which makes actions like exploration, planning, and project development more difficult, while private investment is also constrained due to an uncertain political and business environment. While there have been some improvements, regulations keep

[37] UN World Tourism Organization. 2014. *Responding to Climate Change – Tourism Initiatives in Asia and the Pacific*. Madrid.
[38] Government of Indonesia, MEMR. *Ministerial Regulation No. 10/2017, Ministerial Regulation No. Ministerial Regulation No. 12/2017, Ministerial Regulation No. 49/2017 and Ministerial Regulation No. 50/2017*. Jakarta.

PLN's electricity tariffs below cost recovery, consequently resulting in a dependence on MOF subsidies, straining not only the energy sector but the financial health of the Indonesian government.

The Indonesian constitution requires the government to control the energy sector, but the absence of an independent body to transparently recommend tariffs, review investments, oversee PLN procurement and operations, provide policy advice, and evaluate whether the private sector or SOEs should build new infrastructure stunts the sector. With changing technologies and political circumstances, regulatory bodies globally are often evolving to play a significant role in modernizing the electricity system through regional trade, renewable energy technologies, and smart grid technology deployment. Yet plans developed in Indonesia's RPJMN for this reform have not been implemented.

Equitable development of the energy sector is important to increase economic opportunities and improve health and access to education for all Indonesians. Regional disparities in access to and reliability of fuels and electricity impede the success of the entire country. Indonesia has made impressive progress in increasing the share of the population with access to electricity from 91.2% in 2016 to 98.86% in 2019, with a goal of reaching 100% electrification of the country by 2021.[39] Nevertheless, many electrified regions do not receive 24 hours of electricity per day nor have access to other modern sources of energy. These are the realities, especially in Eastern Indonesia, where dilapidated or non-existent infrastructure impedes the development of public health, education, and the alleviation of poverty. The significant number of households without electricity, approximately 2.3 million at the end of 2018, will be the costliest to supply as the majority of them are located in remote locations. Education on the benefits of increased electrification and training to ensure the sustainability of energy technology is crucial to ensure success in sustaining these achievements.

The use of liquefied petroleum gas (LPG) for cooking in Indonesia has increased rapidly, with more than 70% of households now using the fuel, a large shift from kerosene. However, access is unequal, and an estimated 14.9 million households, many in eastern provinces, still use biomass such as firewood. These traditional sources contribute to health and environmental problems, such as premature death and deforestation. Fiscal and implementation policies are lacking to promote clean fuels, including the expansion of city gas to households and industrial and commercial customers.

There is gender inequality when considering who is the most vulnerable to a lack of energy access and environmental degradation, as women typically are responsible for using resources to provide for the household, from harnessing and using fuels for cooking, to other typical domestic labor that requires lighting. However, this means women, who generally have knowledge of efficient resource management and practices at the household and community level, are best positioned to lead a paradigm shift towards more sustainable energy use. Educating and retaining an educated workforce that ensures increased female participation will continue to improve the quality of life for all Indonesians.

The COVID-19 pandemic has caused an unprecedented, multidimensional, cross-sectoral crisis in Indonesia. Conventional sources of growth, such as relying on a large pool of low-cost labor for competitiveness, may not be reliable in a global context of increased protectionism, shifting global value chains, and rapid technological change. Tackling the underlying constraints across sectors will be critical for a robust recovery in the medium term. This includes developing sufficient human capital; establishing the institutional and physical infrastructure

---

[39] Government of Indonesia, MEMR. 2019. *Growing by 3% Per Year, Electrification Ratio in 3rd Quarter Reaches 98.86%.* Jakarta; and Price Waterhouse Coopers (PWC). 2017. *Power in Indonesia—Investment and Taxation Guide.* Jakarta.

necessary for a rapid economic recovery; and making Indonesia more resilient to crises, climate change risks, environmental degradation, and energy security. As Indonesia recovers from the impact of COVID-19, boosting productivity, competitiveness, and resiliency by creating a more enabling business environment requires addressing regulatory bottlenecks, cumbersome licensing and permitting processes, and inconsistent application of national regulations across different local jurisdictions. The actions are crucial to improving access to finance for needed infrastructure in the energy sector.

Electric Power Subsector

Generation. In 2019, electricity generation capacity reached 62.8 GW. By resource type, coal dominates the mix at 50.7%, followed by gas at 26%, hydropower at 7%, oil at 7.4%, geothermal at 3.0%, biomass at 2.7%, wind and biogas at 0.2% each, solar at 0.1%, and a small amount of waste-to-energy (footnote 32).

The Bali, Java, and Madura regions together encompass 40 GW or 62% of Indonesia's capacity for approximately 60% of the country's population. The next most extensive system is on the island of Sumatra, with 8.6 GW, followed by Kalimantan and Sulawesi (footnote 34). These regions comprise about 90% of Indonesia's energy needs.[40] The rest of Indonesia's generating capacity is across 600 isolated systems. While many of the provinces that have achieved 99% electrification will experience slowing electricity demand growth, the RUPTL 2019–2028 reports that five out of the six provinces on the island of Sulawesi, in addition to the provinces of East and West Nusa Tenggara, East Kalimantan, West Sumatra, and Yogyakarta, will have growing electricity demand.

On the whole, the Indonesian government favors energy independence and lowest-cost energy as an overriding philosophy for managing the country's energy mix. However, the government has not taken into account externalities when assessing costs. As such, coal and diesel power plants continue to enjoy priority deployment, with a young and growing fleet of coal power plants; the government has undervalued Indonesia's high potential for renewable energy investment. For specific types of electricity generation, the government proposed a regionally focused approach to development. Although promoted for decades, in order to develop under-electrified regions, plans were outlined in 2018 for fossil fuel power plants to be developed near the source of extraction, particularly in Sumatra, Kalimantan, Sulawesi, and Papua.[41] This is part of an expansion program launched in 2016 to develop 35,000 MW of capacity by 2029. As of 2019, the program has completed 19% of its goal.

Transmission and Distribution. Maintaining and extending the transmission and distribution network for electricity is paramount to ensuring reliable and accessible energy across the archipelago. Increasing development in energy generation supply needs to be complemented with adequate transmission and distribution infrastructure to improve the performance of the entire energy sector. PLN has a de-facto monopoly over transmission and distribution. Therefore, the burden of financing required upgrades and new construction of transmission falls to PLN. The agency has increased investment from $1.8 billion in 2016 to $4.9 billion in 2019, and has pledged additional investments of around $14 billion for future construction of new substations and transmission and distribution networks between 2021 and 2024.[42]

A 2015 policy introduced power wheeling, which allows IPPs and private power utilities to use existing PLN transmission and distribution networks in an attempt to increase the durability and speed of supplying additional

40 Institute for Essential Services Reform. 2019. *A Roadmap for Indonesia's Power Sector*. Jakarta.
41 PWC. 2018. *Powerguide 2018*. Jakarta.
42 IEA. 2020. *Investment in Transmission and Distribution Networks in Indonesia, 2015–2019*. Paris.

generating capacity.[43] However, specific guidelines for the implementation of wheeling still need to be issued. A small number of transmission lines have been built by IPPs in remote areas to connect power plants to PLN substations, but private sector investment is still needed. There is potential for private sector investment in the unregulated, decentralized, mainly off-grid distribution options that will be important in achieving universal and reliable electrification (footnote 33).

The deterioration of distribution network equipment in oversupplied areas, particularly on Java, should be addressed to support improved reliability. Improved distribution, including an extension of low and medium voltage networks and installation of transformers and services connections, feeders, customer meters and circuit breakers, will reduce overloading and address blackout and system downtime issues. This is important to avoid disruption in the system and in those areas that are newly reaching electrification. It is estimated that PLN's expenditures for distribution upgrades will be $3 billion for distribution upgrades between 2021 and 2024.

PLN is keen to improve overall power sector performance through the introduction of efficient network equipment to reduce technical losses, including the implementation of live-line maintenance. PLN has been rapidly increasing the construction of new network equipment. At the end of 2019, the corporation controlled close to 59,000 ckm of transmission lines and approximately 980,000 ckm of distribution lines across more than 600 isolated grids and eight major networks (footnote 32). The government will focus on constructing transmission networks and substations, targeting an additional 19,069 km and 38,607 MVA of each respective technology over the next five years.[44] The RUPTL 2019-2028 has outlined its network development as shown in Table 1.

Table 1: Network Development Planning

Development Plan	RUPTL 2018–2027	RUPTL 2019–2028
Transformer Load in Substations	151,424 MVA	127,161 MVA
Length of Transmission Network	63,855 ckm	54,160 ckm
Length of Distribution Network	526,391 ckm	407,393 ckm
Number of Customers	25,496,000	22,987,000
Transformer Load in Substations	151,424 MVA	127,161 MVA

ckm = circuit kilometer; MVA = megavolt-ampere; RUPTL = Rencana Usaha Penyediaan Tenaga Listrik (Electricity Power Supply Business Plan).
Source: RUPTL, 2019–2028.

Additional network equipment investment will need to be targeted in underserved communities. ADB support focuses on extending and strengthening the transmission and distribution system in emerging regions. The $600 million Electricity Grid Strengthening–Sumatra Program project includes the reconstruction and installation of new transmission and low and medium voltage distribution lines to support the development of utility-scale new and renewable energy and smart grid pilot projects in the region. Additionally, this project requires additional distribution transformers to be procured on the island of Sumatra with the goal to increase customer base and electricity sales, while minimizing customer complaints and boosting the competency of PLN staff to support the additional generation capacity.

---

[43] Wheeling is defined as transportation of electric energy (megawatt-hours) from within an electrical grid to an electrical load outside the grid boundaries; Government of Indonesia, MEMR. 2015. *Ministerial Regulation 1/2015*. Jakarta.
[44] TEMPO. 2020. *MEMR Targets Additional 8,823 MW of Power Plants*. Jakarta.

Improving grid reliability will be the focus in Eastern Indonesia in particular, where network expansion and new and renewable energy are paramount to the development of the region. ADB is supporting the government through numerous initiatives in Eastern Indonesia. ADB is financing the Electricity Grid Development Program to give a $600 million loan to increase the number of customers connected, increase electricity sales, and minimize interruptions by installing new transmission lines, distribution lines, transformers, and smart grid pilots in Sulawesi and Nusa Tenggara.

Electrification and access. Reaching 100% national electrification is a key goal of the government. While the target is nearly reached, at approx. 98.86% by year-end 2019, the remaining households will be the costliest to supply given their remote location (footnote 39). Difficulties in acquiring upfront capital has constrained the public sector. Frameworks are being introduced to relieve the financial burden from PLN to reach the final target by supporting the acceleration of private small-scale electricity supply businesses for rural electrification.[45] Introduction of nonsovereign players is an opportunity for Indonesia to explore economies of scale and other lower cost alternatives. Electricity access is not equal by region; as of 2019, only 15 out of 34 provinces have reached over 99.0% (footnote 31). The 100% target does not specify the tier of electrification, and further development is needed to reach uninterrupted electricity for all.

Electrification has been achieved principally through extending existing grids, though there has also been some construction of new microgrids, and provision of individual solar home systems. Generation options for microgrids include diesel, solar, and increasingly small-scale hydropower. Determining least-cost electrification involves an analysis of the lowest cost of energy at a specific location, taking into account geography, climate, and factors such as economies of scale for capital costs, technology suitability, and other operations and maintenance expenditures. Energy storage options should be considered for reliability but balanced with financial realities. Sustainably electrifying the country should consider social and economic aspects such as increasing public awareness about the long-term benefits of electricity. Vocational training around project implementation and longevity should also discuss environmental and health benefits, increased access to income and education, and include targeted opportunities for women and indigenous populations. Other socioeconomic considerations such as ensuring an individual household's ability to pay for connection and incentives to ensure longevity of household systems are paramount for success.

Renewable Energy. Recognizing the potential for large-scale development of renewable energy to meet national renewable energy targets, the government introduced various laws in the late 2010s. However regulations introduced in 2017 mandated tariffs, risk allocation, and ownership models for renewable energy projects that ultimately deterred investment.[46] Since then, key stakeholders, including members of government, IPPs, and legal and financial institutions, have mobilized to introduce updated legislation to facilitate renewable energy deployment. While more needs to be done on the policy side, the government has taken action to ease development regulations, reduce contractual risk, and prepare the power grid to be able to accommodate new, renewable, and variable energy, by proposing required transmission and distribution updates and advanced metering and smart grid technology.

Pricing and Subsidies. Presently, PLN cannot recover its full cost of supply with revenue from electricity tariffs alone. Tariff setting requires the concurrence of the legislature. In 2014, the government re-introduced an automatic tariff adjustment mechanism and moved several consumer classes to what it considered to be

---

[45] Government of Indonesia, MEMR. 2016. *Ministerial Regulation No. 38/2016.* Jakarta.
[46] Government of Indonesia, MEMR. 2017. *Ministerial Regulation No. 50/2017.* Jakarta

nonsubsidized tariffs. However, ahead of presidential elections in April 2019, the tariff adjustment mechanism was suspended and tariffs frozen at the end of 2018. Government subsidies, other cash compensation, and capital injections are provided to fiscally support PLN to avoid default on its obligations. This government support is the principal reason why PLN enjoys the same investment-grade credit rating as the government.

The regular electricity subsidies are calculated based on the difference in the estimated cost of supply and the subsidized tariffs for low-income consumers. The national budget allocated subsidies to approximately 40 million customers with 450 and 900 VA connections in 2019.[47] In 2019 the Minister of Energy announced that tariffs would increase in 2020 for 12 nonsubsidized customer groups, though at the time of writing this had not occurred, although the tariff adjustment mechanism had been reactivated. [48]

Peaking in 2019 at Rp356 trillion, fossil fuel subsidies have steadily increased since totaling Rp103.11 trillion in 2017, accounting for approximately 3% of overall GDP (footnote 22). Subsidies remain fixed for diesel and indirectly for RON88 gasoline outside of the Java-Madura-Bali region to ensure that the One-Price-Policy of the fuel is enforced. Used for household cooking, 3 kg LPG cylinders are priced at a subsidized rate of Rp4,250/kg (larger 5.5-kg and 12-kg cylinders are officially not subsidized). This subsidized rate has remained unchanged since 2007. In comparison, the full cost of LPG is Rp8,529/kg (footnote 33). This difference has inevitably fueled a significant LPG subsidy, which has been Rp30–40 trillion in recent years, or 1.5–2.0% of the Indonesian state budget. Electricity subsidies peaked from Rp101.2 trillion in 2013, accounting for 8.8% of national government spending (footnote 34). By 2017, the subsidy fell to Rp45.7 trillion but it has slowly again rising to Rp62 trillion planned in the 2020 state budget (as of 2019).

Further subsidy reform would greatly benefit the entire state of Indonesia's fiscal growth as many are mistargeted: Electricity and fuel subsidies, for instance, disproportionally benefit higher income households. Furthermore, SOEs are unable to keep up with low-cost technology changes due to hindered access to foreign investment. Alleviating financial strain would help PLN focus more on necessary infrastructure upgrades that will improve operational performance and likely attract additional private investment. The MSOE has requested that SOEs use funds from private markets, yet some SOEs face constraints, such as borrowing limits and high debt-to-equity ratios.[49] Facilitating PPP implementation would open up opportunities for SOEs to access lower-cost technology through purchasing cheaper and more sustainable energy from IPPs, particularly for energy generation, transmission and distribution, wheeling, and other expenditures specifically related to reaching 100% electrification.

There is ample evidence for institutional reform in subsidies to support the financial viability of PLN while supporting the development of new and renewable energy. PLN is taking proactive steps to address these issues by implementing innovative digital payment mechanisms, but more needs to be done. Across industries, studies show that subsidies are poorly targeted to customers who are adequately equipped to pay, resulting in approximately Rp19.7 trillion in lost revenue from customer inability to pay (footnote 33). Furthermore, in an ADB cost analysis of a feasibility study for a TransJakarta electric vehicle bus transition, it was found that if the heavily polluting diesel fuel subsidy was allocated to the electricity cost of charging electric buses, this lower-emitting transportation option would be the financially viable choice, not even taking into account the social and environmental externalities.

---

[47] *The Jakarta Post.* 2019. 5 things you need to know from Indonesia's 2020 state budget. 17 October.
[48] TEMPO. 2019. *Indonesia to Raise Electricity Tariff in 2020.* Jakarta.
[49] World Bank Group. 2019. *Unlocking the Dynamism of the Indonesian Private Sector: A Country Private Sector Diagnostic.* Washington, DC.

Regulation. Establishing a technically capable regulator to ensure regulatory transparency and best practices across government agencies will set the grounds for significant growth of private market participation. Required capital from sovereign, private, and multilateral institutions is available, but is not used to its full potential given that uncertain frameworks that hinder development and poorly allocate risk are in place. A key role would be to recommend a balance of subsidies, tariffs, investment plans, and other utility performance targets that are collectively consistent. In addition to strong technical competency, the regulator would conduct these tasks transparently and with opportunities for public participation. Excepting Brunei Darussalam and the Lao People's Democratic Republic, neutral planning bodies have been established in countries across the region to ensure that political and utility influence is raised in a fair manner in line with policy and planning objectives, including the final selection of infrastructure assets to be developed.

Energy Efficiency

Energy efficiency is "the first fuel – the fuel you do not have to use – and in terms of supply, it is abundantly available and cheap to extract."[50] As urbanization and demand for electricity increases, especially for air conditioning and other home appliances, energy efficiency is the quickest and least expensive investment to ensure that enough power and electricity is supplied for all.[51] Energy efficiency measures decreased energy use while guaranteeing the same level of delivery; through demand-side management, minimum performance standards, and efficient technology, they lower greenhouse gases and improve economic competitiveness. Current policies in Indonesia are projected to deliver a 2% reduction in energy use by 2025, but Indonesia has an even greater potential of 10% to 35% savings in energy efficiency across residential, municipal, industrial, and transportation sectors (footnote 51).[52] The RUEN targets a reduction in primary energy intensity by 1% per year through 2025. Development of policies and markets for energy efficiency however have not taken off as a sector on a large scale (footnote 51).

Several key issues are constraining the large-scale development of energy efficiency in Indonesia. Project developers and energy service companies (ESCOs) identified access to finance as the top barrier in a 2017 survey (footnote 52). Generally, awareness of attractive financing options from sovereign, private or PPP players for energy efficiency is low. Fundamentally, there is also a lack of reliable baselines to understand energy use metrics and subsequent standards for energy management. The absence of established guidelines and enforcements, including incentives and disincentives, and minimum performance standards, leads to a lack of verification of savings, demand policies for change, risk reduction, and a capacity gap for market entry. Knowledge of and available funding for inexperienced ESCOs is crucial to increase the market and realize financing for easily achievable energy savings across all sectors. In order for the government and SOEs to contract ESCOs, there is a need to bridge this knowledge gap and create capacity to understand the financial aspects to technically inclined government contracting agencies such as the Directorate General of New and Renewable Energy and Energy Conservation to include technical training for financial stakeholders in order to utilize other resources such as the Indonesia Investment Guarantee Fund, to promote ESCO market development.

While more effort is needed to develop energy efficiency measures in Indonesia, there have been some successes. Although 10 appliances, including refrigerators, washing machines, and televisions, failed to receive targeted minimum energy performance standards, Indonesia has mandated them for air conditioners and compact fluorescent light bulbs. In the municipal space, one of the most readily implementable and cost-

---

[50] IEA. 2019. *Energy Efficiency is the First Fuel, and Demand For It Needs to Grow*. Paris.

[51] ADB. 2019. *Indonesia: Policy Drivers for Municipal Energy Efficiency*. Manila.

[52] Asia-Pacific Economic Cooperation. 2018. *Gaps Assessment on APEC Energy Efficiency and Conservation Work toward Fulfilling the Leaders' Energy Intensity Reduction Goal*. Singapore.

effective options is light-emitting diode (LED)-based street lighting, which can deliver energy cost savings and greenhouse gas emissions reductions of up to 70%. In 2017, initial LED streetlighting pilot programs demonstrated up to 50% energy reductions and associated streetlight costs across municipalities in Batang and Semarang.[53] Pilot programs have been proposed in other cities such as Denpasar and Yogyakarta. The government has established several guarantees for energy efficiency and is working with multilateral institutions, including ADB, to further de-risk and support a nascent market.

Energy Resource Subsectors

Geothermal

Featuring the world's most substantial potential geothermal capacity, 28.5 GW, Indonesia is well-positioned to be a world leader of this renewable energy source. However, the country is only currently using 7% of its geothermal potential, with an installed capacity of approximately 2.0 GW as of 2019 (footnote 10). Most of the resource is colocated with demand in the regions of Sumatra and Java, although potential can be found nationwide.

 Geothermal development has been given a high priority in both the RUPTL and RUEN to meet the country's renewable energy target of 23% of primary energy by 2025. Since the Geothermal Law was enacted in 2003, the government has prioritized the development of this resource and is targeting the development of 7.2 GW of capacity by 2025 (footnote 22). The targeted additional geothermal capacity envisaged by the government is ambitious and will require all actors—public and private—to speed up project implementation significantly.

Geothermal power has the potential to be a crucial component for Indonesia to meet its clean energy targets, project development faces several constraints. Notably, project development risk is high as the location-specific resource potential is highly uncertain and unable to be fully quantified before costly drilling. These risk factors stunt the influx of capital required for upfront exploration, resulting in long project development timelines that hinder project construction financing. However, as of 2019, new policies are being introduced to de-risk geothermal project development through easing regulations and providing incentives to the sector to realize geothermal's potential.

The government allocated resources to support the sector through dedicated programs via the Infrastructure Financing for Geothermal Sector, as well as fiscal incentives for developers through various tax deduction possibilities. The infrastructure funds can be used to support investments by SOEs in geothermal exploration and exploitation. In 2017, the government revised its regulations to clarify the terms of access to geothermal development in protected and conservation forest areas. In addition, the sector is starting to implement a new cost-efficient risk-sharing mechanism, funded by the World Bank and the Green Climate Fund, to mitigate geothermal resource risk for both public and private sector enterprises. ADB, along with other development partners, through the Climate Investment Fund, has helped the government and private sector develop geothermal projects, including nonsovereign financing for the development of Sarulla ($250 million), Muara Laboh ($70 million), and Rantau Dedap ($173 million).

---

[53] ADB. 2017. *LED Street Lighting Best Practices: Lessons Learnt from the Pilot LED Municipal Streetlight and PLN Substation Retrofit Project (Pilot LED Project) in Indonesia*. Manila.

Hydropower

As of 2019, hydropower contributes the largest share of renewable energy to the Indonesian electricity mix, 7%, and to the total energy supply, 2.74% (footnote 10). An estimated 94 GW of hydropower potential is distributed nearly ubiquitously across the archipelago (footnote 15). Yet, Indonesia only uses less than 8% of its capacity, with approx. 5.88 GW installed as of 2019.[54]

The government prioritizes hydropower development, as this renewable source can provide long-term, consistent, baseload power to reach the country's 23% renewable energy target. The government has targeted 17.9 GW of capacity additions of large projects by 2025, in conjunction with 3 GW of small hydro projects. The RPJMN 2020–2024 has targeted development in Papua, Sulawesi, and North Kalimantan as key areas to have increasing demand be met through hydropower to support electrification.[55]

While hydropower capacity is planned to double through 2025, development faces many constraints in long-term growth. Important issues need to be considered ahead of the large-scale development of hydropower, particularly land issues. Several projects causing flooding and other environmental degradation in regions that are home to indigenous people and endangered species have met socioeconomic backlashes. Procuring land involves lengthy permitting processes around impact studies and land acquisition permissions, often causing delays and financing obstacles. Furthermore, climate change affecting rainfall patterns poses additional risk to long-term hydropower development and planning.

The government enacted regulations to ease the way for hydropower development in forest conversation areas as there is interest in establishing projects near rivers and other bodies of water to support remote electricity demand. Given the aforementioned issues with large-scale development, there has been significant interest in developing small-scale hydropower as these projects have the opportunity to increase electrification and reliability in isolated areas of Indonesia at lower costs. Furthermore, smaller projects tend to have a reduced impact on the environment and are, therefore, less risky and can be procured more quickly.

Solar Power

Despite the vast potential of solar energy power generation across Indonesia, the scale of the sector has been mostly untapped, with approximately 150 MW of solar capacity installed by end 2019. Solar has an estimated potential of more than 200 GW (footnote 17).

Utility, commercial, and industrial-sized solar photovoltaic projects have a huge opportunity to quickly build economies of scale to support adhering to the renewable energy target of 23% by 2025. The RUPTL 2019–2028 has targeted 908 MW of capacity by 2028. Furthermore, there is significant potential for small-scale solar to contribute as a lower-environmental impact source of rural and improved electricity in remote parts of the country. Solar, with and without storage, can be deployed to ensure further reliability. Solar-storage mini-grid pilot projects are being explored in the planning of reaching 100% electrification.

While established global markets have brought solar energy production prices down to be lower than most conventional sources of energy, Indonesia has yet to access this potential, lagging behind in both technology manufacturing and project development competencies compared to other Association of Southeast Asian Nation (ASEAN) members. Unfavorable risk allocation and contractual requirements have deterred national and

---

54 International Hydropower Association. 2020. *Country Profile Indonesia*. Romford.
55 International Hydropower Association. 2019. *Indonesia promotes hydropower to create the demand for industrial development*. Romford.

international IPPs, whom have the capability to introduce innovative and low-cost solutions, from entering the Indonesian market. One of the primary roadblocks is the country's local content requirement in solar projects. Developing knowledge around global technology options, the realities of manufacturing of project components (modules, inverters, and other balance of system technologies), and the construction, operation, and maintenance of projects is prudent to the bankability of solar projects in Indonesia being on par with international standards, and to further realize similar levels of project capacity.

The lack of consistent and promotive policy to develop renewable energy projects has contributed to the slow uptick of solar energy, despite projections and plans to increase the share of this energy option. Recent progress has been made by the government to support the development of this source, including new policies to provide frameworks for rooftop solar systems (footnote 25) and allowing reservoir surfaces to be used for floating solar.[56] There is also interest in developing domestic resources for battery and other storage technologies to accommodate the intermittency of solar renewable energy. ADB is committed to supporting the government in the development of the solar market, including technical assistance for exploring price incentives for development, least-cost electrification planning featuring solar photovoltaic technology, and the development of a National Solar Park project and concept for least-cost project development to spur the nascent industry in Indonesia. In 2018, ADB provided nonsovereign resources to fund the first large-scale solar projects, including 21 MW in Likupang and North Sulawesi and three 5 MW projects in Lombok, West Nusa Tenggara.

Wind Power

Indonesia has an estimated 61 GW potential capacity of wind energy (footnote 15). The RUPTL 2019–2028 has a target of 1.8 GW by 2025. Although many regions feature wind speeds that are attractive for wind development, it is often reported that Indonesia does not have high enough wind speeds applicable for large scale wind energy projects. However, advanced technology development in the industry, particularly around turbine capacity efficiencies and offshore wind, may make increased capacity possible in regions with low wind speeds or feature high offshore wind speeds. It is also important to note that the cost of wind energy onshore is already more economical than the generation cost for various types of traditional energy (footnote 22). The highest wind speeds, and subsequently the most substantial potential for wind energy, are in South Sulawesi and Nusa Tenggara Timur, provinces that are challenged by energy access, and Java, the island that features the highest demand (footnote 36).

As of 2019, there is no policy specific to the development and support of wind energy, as the RUPTL and RUEN have targeted a higher uptick of other sources of renewable and nonrenewable energy development. The lack of regulation on wind power measurements and design and the existing legal and commercial problems in MEMR Decree No. 50/2017 have stagnated investment from the private sector. Combined with similar issues that plague development of the other renewable energy sources, such as land acquisition and grid stability, major impediments remain to develop a substantial wind energy market.

The total installed capacity of wind energy in Indonesia as of 2019 was 149 MW, consisting of the Tolo 1 Wind Farm, 72 MW developed by Vena Energy, and Sidrap Wind Farm, 75 MW developed by UPC Renewables. Other small scale and noncommercial supplies comprise the remainder. ADB successfully financed the Tolo 1 Wind Farm in South Sulawesi in 2018 with a $120 million loan, supported by the Lead Asia's Private Sector Infrastructure Fund and the Canadian Climate Fund.

---

56 Government of Indonesia, Ministry of Public Works & Housing. 2020. *Ministerial Regulation No. 6/2020.* Jakarta.

Biomass, Bioenergy, Biofuels, and Waste-to-Energy

Indonesia has abundant biomass sources for bioenergy and biofuels, producing approximately 146.7 million tons per year. Regions with the highest potential of biomass sources include Kalimantan, Sumatra, and Sulawesi, but potential is scattered throughout the country.[57] The government has indicated that domestic cultivation and use of biomass will be a critical component of the nation's goal to achieve 23% renewables by 2025. Indonesia's potential for biofuels is approximately 200,000 barrels per day. Estimates for biomass generated electricity are approximately 33 GW, while the installed capacity lies at about 1.7 GW (footnote 15). In 2019, 12.7 million households relied on traditional biomass fuels for cooking. Options for biomass, derived from the vast domestic agricultural and forestry industries, include products from waste, palm oil, bamboo, rubber, wood pellets, sugar mill residue, oil shells, rice husk, cassava, and more.[58] All sources of bioenergy need to consider the socioeconomic balance across sectors, including sustainable land use and low-carbon and least-cost energy generation.

The crop most supported and sought as a commodity is palm oil. Indonesia is the world's largest producer of palm oil, producing over 30 million tons annually.[59] In terms of energy, palm cultivation is predominantly for the creation of biodiesel. However, palm kernel shells, palm fiber, and empty fruit bunches, all derivatives of palm oil production, can be used in a biomass power plant. Furthermore, a waste product in the conversion of crude palm oil is Palm Oil Mill Effluent (POME), a liquid byproduct that can be used for biogas.[60] Palm oil cultivation and use are subject to considerable backlash over deforestation, wildfire, droughts, pollution, and other threats to indigenous populations and biodiversity. These environmental and socioeconomic issues have resulted in many international stakeholders, notably the European Union, reducing or altogether eliminating the use of the commodity. Given these constraints, Indonesia has increasingly supported the required use of biofuels domestically through policies, regulations, and a significant subsidy to protect national interests in the upstream and downstream markets (footnote 22). Since 2018, Indonesia has required 20% biofuel (B20) to be used in all fuel sources to minimize export and support the market. In late 2019, the government announced that in 2020 the new mandate would require a 30% blend. The government has a plan to conduct testing for biodiesel with a 40% mix in 2020.[61]

With Indonesia's large population producing considerable city and municipal waste, there is vast potential and significant interest in pursuing waste-to-energy projects. In 2018, new policy promoted the development of waste-to-energy plants due to them using environmentally friendly technology (footnote 35). Subsequently, in 2019, the government announced plans to develop three waste-to-energy plants in Java and Banten via reverse auction tender.[62] ADB was appointed the transaction adviser to support one of them, the South Tangerang project, in 2020.

Oil

Indonesia is home to 2.5 billion barrels of proven oil reserves and 1.29 billion barrels of potential oil reserves as of 2019 (footnote 10).[63] While Indonesia suspended its Organization of the Petroleum Exporting Countries membership in 2009, it rejoined again in January 2016 before suspending its membership again in November

---

57 BioEnergy Consult. 2019. *Biomass Energy in Indonesia*. Jakarta.
58 Netherlands Programmes for Sustainable Biomass. 2012. *Indonesia–Market opportunities for Bioenergy*. Amsterdam.
59 United Nations Development Programme. 2020. *Indonesia Palm Oil, Country Fact Sheet*. New York.
60 Endro Gunawan. 2017. Utilization of Palm Oil Processing Waste (palm oil mill effluent/POME) as a Biogas Raw Material in Indonesia: Economic and Institution Approach. *Indonesia Center for Agricultural Socio Economic and Policy Studies*. Jakarta.
61 Reuters. 2019. *Indonesia Launches B30 Biodiesel to Cut Costs, Boost Palm Oil*. London.
62 The Jakarta Post. 2019. *Indonesia to Auction Three Waste-to-Energy Projects This Year*. Jakarta.
63 There was a significant drop in the resources shown by MEMR from 2018 to 2019. This is due to the adoption of new parameters for the Petroleum Resources Management System in 2018. Oil reserves that have not been developed are now categorized as contingent resources.

2016. Indonesia hosts nine refineries with a total capacity of 1.2 million barrels of oil produced a day. As of 2019, Indonesia is a net oil importer. It produces a total of 282 million barrels, imports 113 million barrels, and exports 74 million barrels, predominately to the United States, Japan, and Singapore.[64] Indonesia, due in part to limited buffer stocks, is vulnerable to international volatility in prices and availability as oil is vital to domestic energy use, contributing the highest percentage to the primary energy supply, particularly driven by the transport sector.

Most of the accessible oil in Indonesia is in the western half of the archipelago, mainly Sumatra, the Java Sea, East Kalimantan, and Natuna. In 2018, oil production was carried out by international companies, notably Chevron and Mobil, whose total market share exceeded 50%.[65] However, Pertamina has been steadily increasing its share of the upstream Indonesian oil and gas market through taking over operation of expiring production sharing contracts from international oil and gas companies (footnote 65). It is now the largest single oil producer in the country. In terms of downstream, Pertamina is the dominant player responsible for the transportation and distribution network in the country.

For years the sector has stagnated, with oil output 3.7% below target in 2019, the third year of diminishing production due to lack of exploration combined with aging fields with quality issues such as substandard pipes, delayed targets, downtimes, and curtailment.[66] Furthermore, the introduction of a "gross production split" scheme that stipulated unattractive government ownership and unbalanced capital risk allocation to the contractor has deterred foreign and local investment in exploration.[67]

Consumption has been steadily rising while production has been decreasing, prompting the government to support domestic alternatives to imported oil. Indonesia's refining capacity requires updated infrastructure to meet domestic demand for existing products and higher grades of fuels. New regulations are needed, and expected, to ease impediments to attracting additional foreign investment to expand exploration and use new advanced technologies to scale up domestic production. However, global price volatility and changing regulations could continue to add uncertainty and financial instability to the sector for several years to come.

Natural Gas

Indonesia has 49.74 billion barrels of proven reserves and 27.55 billion barrels of potential reserves of natural gas; it produced nearly 3 million standard cubic feet in 2019 (footnote 10). As of 2019, gas was 18.5% of the primary energy supply. The country is the 11th highest producing in the world, and the second largest in the region, after the People's Republic of China. The main locations of gas are offshore near Sumatra, East Kalimantan, Papua, and Natuna (footnote 60). Like oil, new exploration has stagnated and is lacking incentives for further uptake of the sector.

To decrease dependence on imported oil, the government is strategically targeting the country's domestic use of gas by setting a domestic market obligation, investing in distribution infrastructure, and developing policies to encourage development. In 2019, Indonesian-owned companies produced about 60% of total oil and gas in the country. This figure is forecast to rise to 70% by the end of 2020 and 86% by 2050 (footnote 60). Consumption of natural gas is of particular importance to the industrial sector, contributing significantly to fertilizer,

---

64 The International Comparative Legal Guides and Business Reports. 2020. *Indonesia Oil& Gas Regulation*. London.
65 PWC. 2019. *Oil and Gas Guide.* London.
66 Reuters. 2020. *Indonesia's new law to take years to reverse oil and gas output slump.* London.
67 Government of Indonesia, MEMR. 2017. *Ministerial Regulation No. 8/2017.* Jakarta; The Jakarta Post. 2020. *What's wrong with oil and gas exploration in Indonesia.* Jakarta.

petrochemicals, and steel markets. In parallel, the government has a coal bed methane development target of 46 million standard cubic feet per day by 2025.[68]

LNG remains important in the energy sector in Indonesia. The country was once the largest exporter, but it now ranks seventh in the world, exporting 20 million tons of LNG in 2019 (footnote 10).[69] Due to long-term contract obligations and ineffective policies leading to insufficient investment, the sector may experience a slump without proper investment. A gross split scheme, similar to oil, has not attracted the necessary investment to continue growth. ADB is involved in two gas power projects, the Jawa-1 Liquefied Natural Gas-to-Power Project and the Riau Natural Gas Power Project.

Coal

Coal accounts for 37% of the total primary energy supply in Indonesia (footnote 10). The fuel dominates the electricity sector, contributing 60% of the total generation and growing (footnote 17). As of December 2019, coal resources were at an estimated 149 billion tons with 37.6 billion tons of reserves (footnote 10). In 2019, the country produced 616 million tons of coal (footnote 10). In addition to being important domestically, coal is a keystone commodity for international trade; approximately 80% produced domestically is exported overseas, mainly to the People's Republic of China, India, and Japan.

Coal is concentrated in the provinces of East Kalimantan, South Sumatra, South Kalimantan, and Central Kalimantan. Coal activities contribute significantly to the local economies of these provinces. East Kalimantan features reserves of medium-quality coal while Central and South Sumatra basins feature significant resources of low-quality coal reserves.

After decreasing in the early 1990s, the use of coal has been steadily rising in Indonesia since 1995. The majority of Indonesia's coal-fired power plants are under 10 years old. Coal is attractive in power plant development due to the ability to maintain a higher reserve to production ratio of the fuel compared to oil which, in turn, can minimize the account deficit and inflation from oil imports. As the government looks for further innovative solutions to reduce dependence on imported oil, a program is being explored to substitute LPG with dimethyl ether from domestic coal with induction stoves (footnote 15). PLN has slated an additional 27 GW of coal-fired generation in RUPTL 2019–2028, which will increase the share of coal in the electricity mix to 60–65% of electricity capacity.

State decision-making supports policy and incentives to keep the price of coal low to support the domestic industry, sustaining reliance on the commodity as a fuel. Each year MEMR decrees the amount of coal that companies are obliged to supply to domestic buyers through domestic market obligations. Local governance frameworks concerning incentives for coal activities encourages over-mining, resulting in over-production. Further encouraging its use, the government applies a coal price cap of $70 per ton to PLN.[70]

The increase of coal has contributed to environmental degradation and worsening air quality in communities where the fuel is mined and used. Furthermore, PLN has reported a decrease in coal efficiencies of 360 tons/GWh to 520 tons/GWH, indicating the use of lower-quality coal.[71] The artificial price incentives to keep domestic costs depressed are contributing to the financial burden of the state budget's expenditures. Despite these externalities, the use of coal is expected to increase for the foreseeable future.

---

68 Government of Indonesia, MEMR, Director of Various New and Renewable Energy. 2019. *Renewable Energy Development Strategy in Indonesia,* Jakarta.
69 Organization for Economic Co-operation and Development. 2019. *Fossil Fuel Support Country Note.* Paris.
70 Reuters. 2019. *Indonesia plans to keep $70/T coal price cap for PLN, DMO.* London.
71 Institute for Essential Services Reform. 2019. *Indonesia's Coal Dynamics: Toward A Just Energy Transition.* Jakarta.

II Sector Strategy

Government Strategy, Policy, and Plans

Indonesia's broad development goals are outlined in its long-term national development plan for 2005–2025.[72] This plan is divided into four 5-year phases.[73] Long-term goals for the energy sector are outlined in the 2014 KEN, to be implemented in the National Energy Plan (RUEN), which emphasizes resource diversification, environmental sustainability, and maximized use of domestic resources.[74] The policy targets an energy mix by 2025 of oil (25%), gas (22%), coal (30%), and new and renewable energy (23%).[75] Long-term goals for the electricity subsector are in the government's RUKN, with specific investment plans outlined in PLN's rolling RUPTL, updated annually.

Government-led reforms and programs initiated from 2016 till 2020 aimed to: (i) improve sector governance and expand energy production through greater private sector investment and more effective public sector investment; (ii) increase the country's use of domestic resources; (iii) expand renewable energy generation and energy efficiency investments; and (iv) expand access to modern energy for all Indonesians. A particular focus of the strategy was on reaching remote areas of the archipelago, especially the eastern regions, where energy access rates are lowest and where renewable energy options are often the most economically viable.

The government strategy 2020–2024 focuses on shifting from foreign dependence on oil to supporting domestic industries and sources of power, mainly coal, geothermal, hydropower, and electric vehicles. For the foreseeable future, the government will continue to invest in the development of a domestic coal industry that will be the main contribution to Indonesia's energy supply past 2028. The installed capacity of coal is set to nearly double over the next decade. Simultaneously, the Energy and Mineral Resources Minister has announced plans to replace retiring coal plants with new and renewable energy to meet growing demand across the archipelago, indicating national support for meeting energy mix targets.[76] While maximum uptick of regulatory support has been stunted, recent and planned regulations and decrees aim to make clear guidelines and reduce red tape around private sector involvement and land-use for all large-scale renewable energy projects, including geothermal development, rooftop solar, floating solar, and commercial and legal implications for utility-scale solar.[77]

---

72   Government of Indonesia, BAPPENAS. 2005. *National Long-Term Development Plan, 2005–2025*. Jakarta.
73   Government of Indonesia, BAPPENAS. 2015. *National Medium-Term Development Plan, 2015–2019*. Jakarta.
74   Government of Indonesia, National Energy Council. 2014. *National Energy Policy, 2014–2050*. Jakarta.
75   Increased renewables will help the government achieve its emission reduction targets as stipulated in Indonesia's Nationally Determined Contribution to the Paris Agreement of 2015.
76   Reuters. 2020. *Indonesia plans to replace old coal power plants with renewable plants: minister*. London.
77   Eco-Business. 2020. *New renewables bill may give Indonesia chance to move away from coal*. Singapore.

ADB Sector Support Program and Experience

Since 1970, the ADB has financed more than 50 projects and programs with total lending of $5.5 billion for Indonesia's energy sector. With few exceptions, completed loan projects have delivered their expected outputs and achieved their immediate objectives. ADB investments during 1999–2017 included nine approved loans totaling $3.2 billion.

Table 2: ADB Major Public Sector Projects in Indonesia Since 2016

Project Name	Amount ($ million)
Java–Bali Electricity Distribution Performance Improvement Project	50.0
West Kalimantan Power Grid Strengthening Project	49.5
Java–Bali 500-Kilovolt Power Transmission Crossing	224.0
Sustainable and Inclusive Energy Program–Subprogram 1 and 2	1,000.0
Sustainable Energy Access in Eastern Indonesia: Electricity Grid Development Program Results Based Loan	600.0
Electricity Grid Strengthening–Sumatra Program	600.0

Source: Asian Development Bank.

Table 3: ADB Major Private Sector Projects in Indonesia Since 2016

Project Name	Location	Capacity (MW)
Riau 275 MW Combined-Cycle Gas-Fired Power Plant	Sumatra	275
Jawa-1 Liquified National Gas-to-Power	West Java	1,760
Eastern Indonesia Renewable Energy Project Phase 1 Tolo Wind	South Sulawesi	72
Eastern Indonesia Renewable Energy Project Phase 2 One 21 MW Solar	Sulawesi	21
Eastern Indonesia Renewable Energy Project Phase 2-three 7 MW Solar	West Nusa Tenggara	21
Rantau Dedap Geothermal	South Sumatra	90

MW = megawatt.
Source: Asian Development Bank.

Since 2010, ADB has supported the government in its energy reform efforts through a range of technical assistance, predominantly via the Sustainable Infrastructure Assistance Programs–Phase I and II, focused on: (i) a reduction in subsidies in favor of cost-recovery tariffs for fuels and electricity; (ii) price incentives for new and renewable energy including geothermal, wind, and large-scale and rooftop solar energy; (iii) energy efficiency-related policies and programs, including support for ESCOs and appliance standards; (iv) gas sector reform; (v) least-cost electrification planning to support the national electrification program; (vi) pilot testing of carbon capture and storage, (vii) electricity market restructuring, and (vii) electric vehicle transportation, including feasibility studies for select routes. In 2020, ADB prepared a White Paper, Independent Assessment of Indonesia's Energy Infrastructure Sector, to highlight key constraints and directions for possible reform in the energy sector.

The government has been actively seeking greater financing for energy infrastructure development since 2015. Under a direct lending modality with a sovereign-backed guarantee, multilateral and bilateral lenders can lend directly to state-owned companies in the energy sector without going through the MOF. This aims to speed up financing for projects. PLN is working closely with ADB to implement results-based lending programs to strengthen the electricity grid and overall power sector in various parts of the country. ADB's policy-based lending to the government in addition to its nonsovereign lending to the private sector for the financing of projects will also continue.[78]

Other Development Partner Support

ADB has coordinated support with numerous other multilateral and bilateral agencies in the energy sector. Development Partners include the World Bank, Japan International Development Cooperation Agency (JICA), Kreditanstalt für Wiederaufbau (KfW), Agence Française de Développement (AFD) and United States Agency for International Development (USAID). The governments of Australia, New Zealand, the United Kingdom, Canada, Netherlands, Norway, and Finland have also been involved.

The Sustainable and Inclusive Energy Program, subprograms 1, 2, and the forthcoming 3 policy-based loans have been the key tool for donor coordination on the larger energy agenda in Indonesia, inviting participation from the ASEAN Infrastructure Fund, KfW, JICA, AFD, the World Bank, and the Clean Energy Fund under the Clean Energy Financing Partnership Facility at ADB. Energy sector round tables focusing on key areas, in particular for geothermal, occur frequently and include additional bilateral actors such as USAID, AFD, JICA, KfW, New Zealand, UK, and the World Bank.

Table 4: Major Development Partners and Programs 2016–2019

Project Name	Year Approved	Amount ($ million)
Asian Development Bank		
Sustainable and Inclusive Energy Program, Subprogram 3	2020 (pending)	400.00
Sustainable Energy Access in Eastern Indonesia: Power Transmission Project	2020 (pending)	300.00
Sustainable Energy Access in Eastern Indonesia: Electricity Grid Development Program (Phase 2) Results-Based Loan	2020 (pending)	600.00
Geothermal Power Generation Project	2020	300.00
Sustainable and Reliable Energy Access Program RBL	2019	300.00
Sustainable Infrastructure Assistance Program Phase 2	2018	30.00
Sustainable and Inclusive Energy Program, Subprogram 2	2017	400.00
Pilot Carbon Capture and Storage Activity in the Natural Gas Processing Sector	2016	1.85

continued on next page

---

[78] The private sector is to undertake the bulk of the capacity expansion.

Table 4 continued

Project Name	Year Approved	Amount ($ million)
Private Sector Operations Department		
Riau Natural Gas Power Project	2018	167.90
Jawa-1 Liquified Natural Gas-to-Power Project	2018	305.05
Eastern Indonesia Renewable Energy Project Phase 2	2018	40.17
Rantau Dedap Geothermal Power Project (Phase 2)	2018	227.50
Eastern Indonesia Renewable Energy Project Phase 1	2017	120.80
Tangguh Liquefied Natural Gas Expansion Project	2016	400.00
Muara Laboh Geothermal Power Project	2016	109.25
KfW		
Sustainable hydropower 2	2017	€225.00
Sustainable hydropower 1	2017	€85.00
World Bank		
Indonesia Geothermal Resource Risk Mitigation Project	2019	465.00
Indonesia's Infrastructure Finance Development	2017	8.28
Geothermal Energy Upstream Development	2017	104.00
Power Distribution Development Program	2016	1,450.00
Indonesia Energy Sector Development Policy Loan	2016	500.00
Japan International Cooperation Agency		
Hululais Geothermal Power Plant Project	2016	6.00
New Zealand		
New Zealand support for training in Indonesian Geothermal Sector	2018	
New Zealand support for accelerating geothermal development in Indonesia	2017	
United Kingdom		
Indonesia Renewable Energy	2019	€13.50
United States Agency for International Development (USAID)		
Indonesia Clean Energy Development 2	2020	
USAID Sustainable Energy for Indonesia's Advancing Resilience	2020	35.00
Gesellschaft fuer Internationale Zusammenarbeit		
Electrification through Renewable Energy	2017	
1,000 Islands – Renewable Energy for Electrification Program	2017	
Association of Southeast Asian Nations-German Energy Programme	2016	

Source: Asian Development Bank.

ADB Sector Forward Strategy

ADB's CPS, 2020–2024 is consistent with the priorities of the government under its RPJMN 2020–2024 to support inclusive, competitive, and sustainable development. It is geared toward helping Indonesia emerge stronger from the COVID-19 pandemic by focusing on three strategic pathways: (i) improving well-being by strengthening the health care system, expanding social protection, advancing educational quality in an equitable manner, and developing workforce skills; (ii) accelerating the economic recovery by supporting economic policy and structural reforms, domestic resource mobilization, financial market deepening and inclusion, and the development of high-quality infrastructure; and strengthening resilience by supporting climate change mitigation and adaptation measures, environmental sustainability and green recovery, disaster risk management and finance, and water and food security. ADB aims to continue to be an effective partner for Indonesia over the term of the CPS for 2020–2024 by working to overcome potential barriers to future growth and assisting the government's response to COVID-19.

ADB's energy sector strategy in Indonesia will support Indonesia's progress towards achieving the Sustainable Development Goals (SDGs) on clean and affordable energy (SDG7) and support the CPS goal to provide sustainable energy access to all Indonesians as a key outcome indicator, towards which ADB provides lending and nonlending support to the government along with technical expertise on energy policy reform and energy infrastructure. ADB's energy sector support will strive to enable the government's green recovery response by prioritizing clean and renewable energy investments, and energy efficiency measures.

Following the One ADB approach, the energy sector knowledge plan will promote cross-fertilization of knowledge between sovereign and nonsovereign operations, and across sector and themes.[79] ADB intends to facilitate a successful and sustainable COVID-19 response considering all Indonesians. ADB will work with stakeholders to develop government and private sector initiatives towards improved gender outcomes, and help the poor and vulnerable recover from COVID-19. Strengthening overall energy sector governance and institutions through specifically enhancing regional cooperation and integration is paramount to improving local and regional economic development and human capital, especially in rural and island villages. Stimulating government planning, job creation, and private investment opportunities are key areas of foci for ADB support to these communities across the archipelago. ADB will promote digitalization and technological transformation in the energy sector, including leveraging data and advanced analytics for energy infrastructure planning, monitoring, and improvement.

ADB is targeting technical assistance to formulate policies and plans aimed at triggering an environmentally sustainable COVID-19 green recovery path that includes access to least-cost reliable and sustainable forms of electricity across the archipelago to support 100% electrification. Particularly, ADB will embed climate change mitigation and adaptation measures in its infrastructure investments and support Indonesia's nationally determined contribution goal of 23% of energy supply coming from renewable sources by 2025. ADB's support will center on policy reforms toward stronger energy sector governance, clean energy, and energy efficiency, and private sector participation. Investment will focus on sustainable power generation, power transmission systems, and electricity grids. ADB will use new digital technologies in its operations, such as grid automation technologies, smart grids and meters, and active remote sensing systems (LIDAR) to improve survey and planning processes for the operation and maintenance of energy assets. ADB will facilitate the promotion of PPPs to mobilize

---

79   ADB. 2018. *ADB Launches Strategy 2030 to Respond to Changing Needs of Asia and Pacific.* Manila.

investments through leverage of sovereign and nonsovereign modalities to create opportunities and improve the bankability of these type of projects including energy efficiency, waste-to-energy development and low-emission transport schemes.

ADB will support Indonesia to realize its geothermal potential, develop large-scale use of its solar and wind resources, and boost gas-fired power generation infrastructure to provide backup capacity for intermittent use of renewable energy and the replacement of diesel. It will promote private sector investment in low-carbon initiatives, including technologies that enable the efficient use of renewable energy, and provide knowledge and capacity support to the newly established Environmental Trust Agency. It will help mobilize domestic and international climate finance and establish market-based carbon mechanisms. Additional support will be provided to develop municipal energy efficiency programs and a feasibility study for electric vehicle public transport. Also planned is a national solar park project to develop the least-cost concept for the development of utility-scale solar across the nation. ADB's private sector operations will support LNG production and supply in Eastern Indonesia, geothermal exploration and development, and gas-to-power, wind power, and solar photovoltaic projects. Given that sector policies underpin project outcomes and enable private sector investment, ADB's energy sector strategy, as elaborated in the CPS, aims to deploy policy-based lending, project financing, and results-based lending in a mutually reinforcing way.

III Energy Sector Road Map and Results Framework

Country Sector Outcomes		Country Sector Outputs		ADB Sector Operations	
Outcomes with ADB Contributions	**Indicators with Targets and Baselines**	**Outputs with ADB Contributions**	**Indicators with Incremental Targets**	**Planned and Ongoing ADB Interventions**	**Main Outputs Expected from ADB Contributions**
Sustainable energy access achieved for all Indonesians.

Construction, upgrading, and expansion of energy infrastructure

For provision of electricity and gas.

Increased use of electricity generated from new and renewable sources.

Strengthened and upgraded transmission and distribution systems.

Promotion of innovative low-carbon technologies such as electric transport. | Percentage of households with an electricity connection increased from 98.3% in 2018 and to 99% by 2023 (2014 baseline 84.3%).

Share of new and renewable energy reaching 8.6% in 2018 to 23% by 2025 (2014 baseline 5.3%).

Share of gas contribution to the primary energy supply increased to 19% (2014 baseline 17%).

Share of new and renewable energy electricity capacity increased to 15% of the generation capacity mix in 2018 (2014 baseline 12%).

Transmission line length increased by over 9% to 53,300 ckm in 2018 (2016 baseline 44,100 ckm).

Distribution line length increased by over 3% to 949,000 ckm in 2018 (2016 baseline 889,000 ckm).

Deployment of 400,000 units of electric vehicles by 2025. | Sector policy reforms conducted for sustainable and inclusive energy access.

The reach, reliability, and efficiency of the nation's electricity grid strengthened.

Capacity from clean sources of energy increased.

Electric public bus transport introduced. | Percentage of private sector participation in installed electricity generation capacity increased to 28% in 2018 (2014 baseline 23%).

Number of PLN customers increased by over 5% per year to 72 million in 2018 (2016 baseline 64 million).

PLN energy sales, increased by 3% per year to 235 TWh in 2018 (2016 baseline 216 TWh).

Generation capacity from clean energy sources increased by 1 GW by 2023.

50 diesel buses replaced by electric buses by 2023.

Reduce households dependent on traditional fuels (2018 baseline 12.7 million households) through introduction of clean cooking options. | **Planned key activity areas:**
(i) Policy and regulatory reforms
(ii) Power generation
(iii) Electricity transmission and distribution
(iv) Efficiency improvement
(v) Renewable energy
(vi) Electric vehicles

Pipeline projects with estimated amounts:
(i) Sustainable and Inclusive Energy Program subprogram 3 ($400 million)
(ii) Electricity Grid Development Program Phase 2 ($600 million)
(iii) Power Generation Sector Project ($375 million)
(iv) Sustainable and Reliable Energy Access Program ($600 million)

Ongoing projects with approved amounts:
(i) Electricity Grid Strengthening Program ($1,200 million)
(ii) Electricity Grid Development Program ($600 million) | **Planned key activity areas:**
(i) Market-based pricing of fuels and power
(ii) Improved governance with the establishment of an energy regulator
(iii) Streamlined project licensing and permitting for energy projects
(iv) Access to clean energy increased
(v) 3 million new customers connected to the electricity grid by 2023
(vi) System Average Interruption Duration Index reduced by 15% (from a 16 hour/customer) baseline in 2018)

Pipeline projects:
(i) Improved sector governance
(ii) Existing transmission and distributions systems strengthened and expanded
(iii) Generation capacity added from clean energy sources: geothermal (1 GW), and gas (100 MW)

Ongoing projects:
(i) Geothermal Power Development Project ($300 million)
(ii) Jawa-1 Liquified Natural Gas-to-Power ($305 million)
(iii) Riau Gas Project ($175 million) |

Source: Asian Development Bank.

Appendix

Problem Tree for the Energy Sector

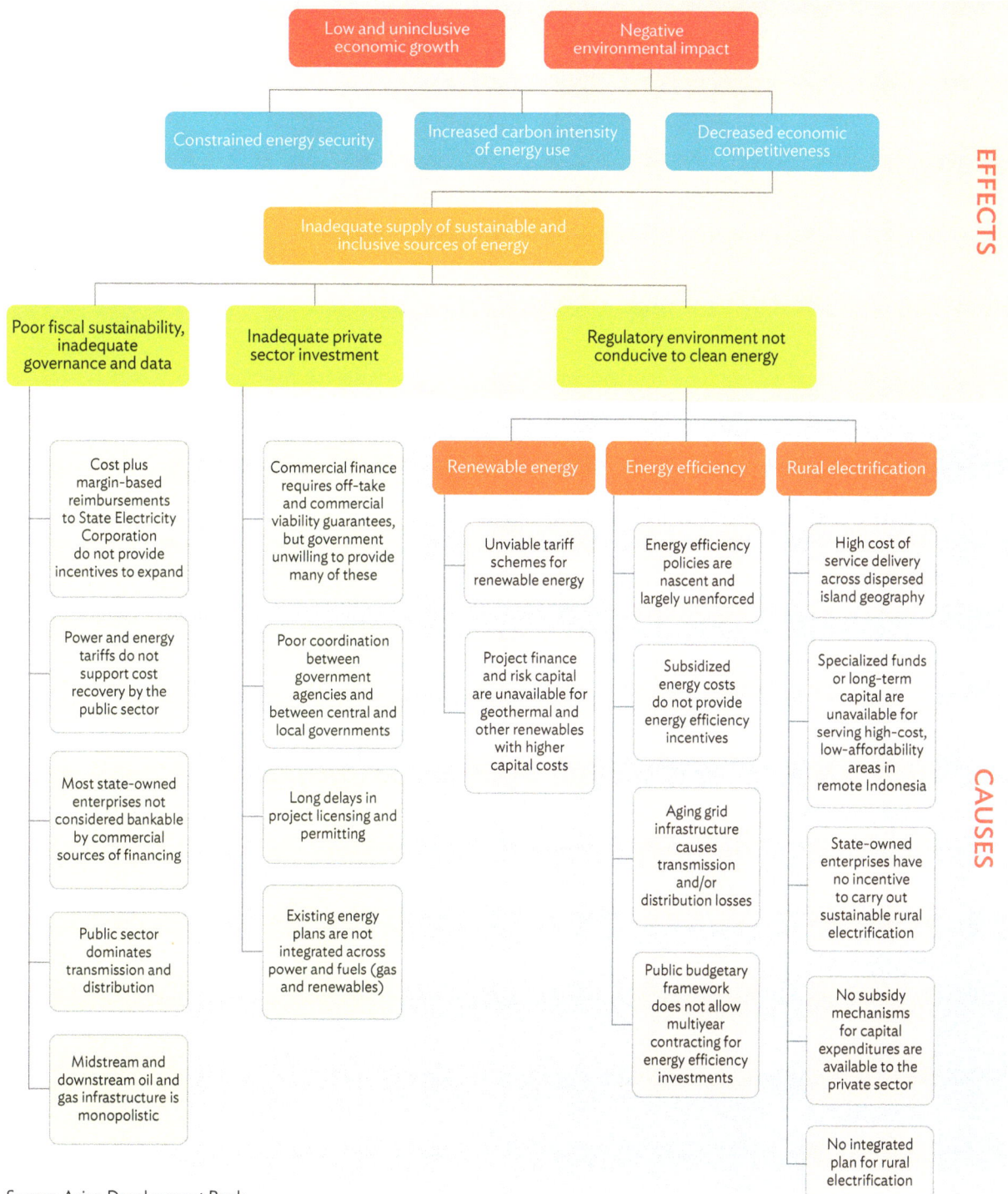

Low and uninclusive economic growth

Negative environmental impact

EFFECTS

Constrained energy security

Increased carbon intensity of energy use

Decreased economic competitiveness

Inadequate supply of sustainable and inclusive sources of energy

Poor fiscal sustainability, inadequate governance and data

Inadequate private sector investment

Regulatory environment not conducive to clean energy

Renewable energy

Energy efficiency

Rural electrification

CAUSES

Cost plus margin-based reimbursements to State Electricity Corporation do not provide incentives to expand

Power and energy tariffs do not support cost recovery by the public sector

Most state-owned enterprises not considered bankable by commercial sources of financing

Public sector dominates transmission and distribution

Midstream and downstream oil and gas infrastructure is monopolistic

Commercial finance requires off-take and commercial viability guarantees, but government unwilling to provide many of these

Poor coordination between government agencies and between central and local governments

Long delays in project licensing and permitting

Existing energy plans are not integrated across power and fuels (gas and renewables)

Unviable tariff schemes for renewable energy

Project finance and risk capital are unavailable for geothermal and other renewables with higher capital costs

Energy efficiency policies are nascent and largely unenforced

Subsidized energy costs do not provide energy efficiency incentives

Aging grid infrastructure causes transmission and/or distribution losses

Public budgetary framework does not allow multiyear contracting for energy efficiency investments

High cost of service delivery across dispersed island geography

Specialized funds or long-term capital are unavailable for serving high-cost, low-affordability areas in remote Indonesia

State-owned enterprises have no incentive to carry out sustainable rural electrification

No subsidy mechanisms for capital expenditures are available to the private sector

No integrated plan for rural electrification

Source: Asian Development Bank.

www.ingramcontent.com/pod-product-compliance
Lightning Source LLC
Chambersburg PA
CBHW041432270326
41935CB00025B/1860